Musings, Meditations, Melodies.

Poetry

Tamar Shengelia

BookLeaf
Publishing

India | USA | UK

Made with ❤ on the BookLeaf Publishing Platform

www.bookleafpub.in

www.bookleafpub.com

Dedication

To my brilliant son Nick, love forever.
To my loving and always supporting husband, Raj.
To my family, Mom- Dali and Dad- Avto,
from their forever grateful daughter.
And lastly to our Doggo Buster for walking me daily
and letting me enjoy the nature and surroundings.

Preface

These poems grew from quiet soil of reflection - from the slow turning of seasons, the tender shimmer of petals in sunlight, pitter-patter of rain in my garden, fragrance of the world in bloom and decay. Each poem is a meditation, a listening to nature: to flowers that speak in colors, to winds that hum in mysterious tongues, to the pulse of the time and roots beneath our feet.

They draw from nature, memory, songs and myths, from the small revelations that arise when one pauses long enough to see how beauty and loss entwine:
rain sings, and the earth remembers; roses, irises, nasturtiums, immortelles, lilacs - each bloom in thought, in dream, becoming a mirror, a symbol, a melody reborn through silence and feeling.

Together they form a journey inward and outward, from visible to felt, from what passes to what endures.

These are my musings, meditations and melodies - offerings of stillness, of wonder, of becoming.

Acknowledgements

My gratitude to the quiet hours and the voices of nature
that shaped these poems: the rain on windowsills, the
faithful moon, the fields of poppies and daisies, the
winding paths in parks, and the songs of my homeland.

To my family, for their patience and love; and to my
friends and fellow poets in the Facebook poetry circles
who listened, read, offered feedback, and encouraged me
along the way.

And to my son, my alpha and omega, the reason I started
again to write, whose laughter and dreams, victories and
growth, remain my truest music.

1. Alchemy of Reading.

To browse the stalls, stumble on a book,
Open, turn the pages at a random
And read, read gulping phrases,
Devouring sentences, skimming surface
Of glossy pages with silver signs and scripts,
Codes that open doors of mind and heart,
In a hurry look and follow the sequences
Of descriptions and thoughts, unimpressed so far...

And then suddenly - a word, a single word
That halts you in the tracks, holds, calls to attention,
Hooks and tags on mind's imagination
And you - the reader, the partaker, maker and conjurer
Of written signs and codes,
Pause and decide – good, this book,
I will read it...
Check for the name of the author,
then continue, back to reading.

Dreaming, playing, soaring, being that someone else,

Feeling anew and the same...
And every day, every single day committed to the story,
or poem, or novel, or play at hand, - you name it,
every time, returning till it is over, till it is read,
and became you, your truth, realization,
your revelation, part-life, part-fantasy,
part only truth, part falsehood,
part reflection, part mirror,
the knowledge that makes up your soul and verse.

Tamar Shengelia
Oct. 10, 2025

2. The Colors We Choose.

Who can right all the wrongs in the World?

Only self - with the beauty seen and recognized.
Your eyes so tired, watch lacking, wanting a word, one
word to lean on...
I don't want to think world defeated by ugliness and
greed, and us in it, -
The decent, feeling, caring people, stuck in rut and dirt,
hurt, searching for the smallest hope...

They say it is the mercy and perfection of the words,
shapes, sounds, fantasies -
the whole artful effort and imagination, that will change
the gray and filth and dreg
into not quite starched, not pristine, but more palatable
colors:
sunshine of smiles, passions, thoughtful ruminations, the
kindness of children,
that infantile perception that denies the existence of all
evils.

Yes, maybe delusional, but so timely, in demand...
So let us erase the grey grease of doubts, polish hopes to
shine,
And paint the colors of disillusionment into bright dyes
–
Into welcoming smiles, proud hopeful, loving.

Tamar Shengelia
Oct. 2, 2025

2. How Much In Heart?

"How much can your heart hold?"- you poised the question.
Of love, care, hope, desperation, fear, levity, doubts?
A crimson-purpled, mighty muscle, stretching like a harmonica,
It cries and sings, belting melodies of a thousand megahertz,
when properly and adequately challenged.
So, darling, don't mess with it!
Don't alter the frequencies it is attuned to:
Truth, only truth, until the last word, last breath.
I promise to produce!

I had paused for a while, absorbing silly nothings –
Hollow pomp, not even circumstance.
To right what is wrong with us and world surround,
Just the 'merde' that casually happens.
I ain't, God forbid, a prophet foretelling end of times...

You and I – mortal, through and through,

And that's the vexing point to rub our noses and gasp at
times in disbelief.
I am no nerd who knows or guesses all the time,
Who is sure of everything that might happen,
Yet keeps her heart at ZERO, -
Afraid to feel, afraid to hurt, weary of overflow
The chalice filled to brim meant exclusively for us,
I am all for tossing the excess aside, mere ballast of the
egos...
And I carry all my meager baggage:
Some knowledge, rudimentary, at best,
feelings sharp, sappy too,
garbage accumulated through the years, -
Greeks so aptly called it hubris!
Dense and tense, condensed, with P – density,
Packed to its highest weight, tons pressed in each square
centimeter,
Lika a spring, coiled, trembling,
Ready to release its accumulated tension
In words, upon the world.

So let the heart hold, stretch, swell with all it gathers -
Love and fury, hope and fear, all the baggage, all the
music of the upper spheres.
Let her release, not squeeze in and break, or keep
vaulted.
Its true frequency of love and hope is ringing off and out,

Until the silences themselves bend and beg to listen.

Tamar Shengelia
Sept.17, 2025

3. Sursum Corda! Lift Your Hearts!

This day - a new beginning,
Lush, warm, glowing with a promise,
Waiting for me to rise and shine,
To spin through my daily orbits
Of chores, tasks and deed,
Small or large –
The same open circuit
Of to-dos and musts.

So, I lift my face, my heart,
To greet a thousand splendid stars,
New starts, alive with promise,
Each one blazing with
A stubborn hope and quiet strength.

Tamar Shengelia
Sept. 9, 2025

4. Suliko / სულიკო

Suliko- **სულიკო** *is a beloved Georgian folk song, its title meaning "soul, little soul." Written by Akaki Tsereteli in 1895 the song expresses deep longing and spiritual yearning. Its haunting melody, often performed by generations of Georgian artists, evokes profound emotional reflection. The lyrics tell of searching for a lost beloved, finding traces in nature's symbols- a rose, a nightingale, the wind.*

სადა ხარ ჩემო სულიკო? Where art thou, my little soul?
Where are you floating, flying,
playing in the upper ethers of teal skies,
my tiny baby soul, of pure joy and sudden tears,
of distant hopes and recollections,
my heart's unadulterated kindness,
my bellyful of smiles and laughter,
bright dreams of happiness!

სადა ხარ ჩემო სულიკო? Where art thou, my little

soul?
Are you faltering, hopping like a fledgling
fallen from its soft oval nest, striving to take to the skies

-

your daring wings spread or tumbling deep
into the ocean's wavy molasses-green,
where time is thick and liquid,
and dolphins – mischievous daughters of the Gods-
whirl you through the lulling streams.

სადა ხარ ჩემო სულიკო? Where art thou, my little
soul?
I call, I wait, I summon you to shore.
Return to my thirsty body, come back,
return with true devotion and the quest,
inhabit heart and chest.
Give me the voice and strength
To be my best!

სადა ხარ ჩემო სულიკო? Where art thou, my little
soul?
I whispered among the beloved graves,
searching in forgotten brambles.
The gold-chested nightingale sang -
And I repeated her lament: Where art thou, my little
soul?
Which side of Eden do you frolic,

Which green lawn from divine pastures?
Or lost in the depth of oblivion,
where disjointed links of shaky time matrices
break and reside, but in trembling inky hearts
of the majestic purple roses?
Reply, respond to my call please, -

სადა ხარ ჩემო სულიკო? Where art thou, my little
soul?
Don't leave me stuck in present!
Questing for my true colors of ultimate identity –
my oneness with the divine,
with these high skies, breeze, and darkness.
She won't reveal herself, my pure little baby soul –
Yet she gurgles, lolls, gambols, smiles,
And sings, and sings.

Tamar Shengelia
Aug. 18, 2025

5. Birds Of Paradise

Drink this cold mountain brook
and feel the frost on your tongue.
Toothache spreads upward,
knocking out the glands and nose,
then freezes the very synapses of the brain.
Drink, gulp more, soothe the pain, seeking oblivion
in these shaded recesses of the overgrown, unlighted
cave.
The tears of the brook, seeping from the dark walls,
dew the velvet moss and stone through,
Leaving white grooves like veins upon your temples.
Perhaps here once stood an ancient Temple
dedicated to some great river god;
Powerful and mighty,
All take their start from brooks, rising up and
Then hiding in the ground and reappearing with swell
and flow.
No way to know, only to surmise.
Yet this place feels auspicious.
Surprise yourself,

succumb to urge, go on your knees, and pray!
Yes, your eyes, your soul, your mind demand it.
Pray to whatever deities, whatever seems most fitting to
explain this harmony,
its astounding sacred beauty
washed by the golden rays of the setting sun.
I usually pray for my home, my family, and my son...so I
will do thus.
In privacy of this enduring peace
hung in an eternity of this moment,
in deep indulgence, I decimate, forget, and toss all
worries -
future, past daily tasks and work, or business.
This holy part of self – the soul of Holi colors,
Embracing all -
All that is umbilically intertwined with thick,
knotted cords of the protruding roots.
The nourishment of Mother Earth...
They are black and dwell deep in the underworld –
Can they not feed and carry us through light?
Yet they are the radicle and source of life, shooting
upward
from below, the magnificence of green giants
with hanging arms, with swaying palms of emeralds,
caressing the songbirds straight from paradise,
that flutter, fly, sing and serenade our hearts.
All this, I know, you see and embrace, my son,

Is a gift, a grace for you to thrive and live,
To find reverence in each moment of this fleeting life-
So diminutive beside the immensity of
Earth, and Cosmos, yet so sacred, radiant,
Meaningful and potent.

Tamar Shengelia
Sept. 8, 2025

6. On A Quiet Eve

On a quiet eve, pose at the windows
and watch as flowers blossom in the garden,
washed by the showers of the rain.
They stand tall and sway
fresh, fragrant, bright,
rinsed off the dust and heat and grime,
and an exhaustion
Of this scorching summer day.

Tamar Shengelia
July 29, 2025

7. Lavender Blue, Lavender Green (singalong)

Lavender Blue, dilly dilly
Lavender Green,
Come hither with me, dilly dilly,
to garden in bloom, dilly dilly – pink, red, and teal.
Blue lavender boughs, dilly dilly,
lavender greens,
lavender blue dilly dilly,
all sway in the breeze!

Daisies and poppies, dilly dilly,
blossom and please,
Teal brushes of mint, dilly dilly,
drip fragrance with ease.

I'll hide, you can seek, dilly dilly,
I won't be hard to find,
Midst lavender purple, dilly dilly,
green-and-blues all entwined!

Come hither, dilly dilly, come
smile, breathe, and play,
The garden's alive, dilly dilly,
in the sunlight a-sway.

Twirling and prancing, dilly dilly,
dressed in yellow and pink,
The girlies romancing, dilly dilly,
laugh, dance, and clink.

Lavender purple, dilly dilly,
lavender blue,
I love you so, dilly dilly,
I love you so true!

Come out to the garden, silly, silly,
dress in color and silk,
Come drink with me, dilly dilly,
laugh,
prance,
and sing!

Lavender blue, dilly dilly,
lavender green,
Life is so short, dilly dilly,
life is so trim!

Come with me, walk willy-nilly
toast life and love,
Oh, lavender purple,
the scent and the charm!

Come dance with me, dilly dilly
kiss, prance, and sing!
Lavender blue, dilly dilly,
lavender green.

Tamar Shengelia
Sept. 6,2025

8. Sunflower Thoughts.

The Sun, relentless, blazing hot, has smooched and
consummated with his persistent warmth
fertile Earth, still dormant,
and she nurtured and unfurled the bright yellow smiles.
Standing proud and tall, heads spinning and following
the radiance of light,
with wide toothy grins and meaty petals, yellow mouths
parted,
ready to devour a day in a single ardent kiss!
They shout and wave at Wind and Rain, calling: We miss
you, miss you too!
Their many-layered hearts, - sunny golden sunflowers
mirror pulse of cosmic love -
Receiving heat, giving away joy, simply being.
Brightness! Lightness! Bliss!
Look at them, their happy faces, and dare to ask:
What is the point of your utter kindness, o, Cosmos,
Earth and Stars?
Here comes the tricky part for us, used to
explanations.

Kindness makes no other sense, but its own pure quality,
in its sincerity of heart and being - just as love and
generosity are...
Rustaveli knew it: to give away, is to become wholesome.
To donate is to be fulfilled. Truly, truly!
Truly, alleluia!
May Thy Will
be done on Earth as in Heaven!

Tamar Shengelia
July 24, 2025

9. Turtles and Shells.

After Aesop – a homage to wisdom of slowness.

Oval bones of laced, stony shells –
A framework of sturdiness and protection.
Well-known in fable, the savoring grass-eaters,
Lackadaisical. The chillaxing ones –
Bent, scaly legs with tiny claws,
Moving one after another down the path,
At their own pace –
Turtle, tortoise, turtle-ish.

Khaki, earthly tones,
A calm, intent gaze
From round, docile agate eyes.
Mouths agape –
Baby-pink tongues whisper
Wisdom of lives lived well – long and peaceful.
Wiry necks stretch, turning
Their serpentine heads,
Blunt noses smell the air

Through vibrating, tiny nostril holes.

Slow, deliberate,
As if time itself bends to their pace –
No haste, no hurry,
Only the quiet art of being.
Slow truly wins the race –
But what race? Why race?
Who would race at all,
when one could simply bask
in sunlight and stillness-
majestic, magnificent, poised –
gazing at the lawn and lakes,
each moment a small eternity
in khaki, green, and gold.

Tamar Shengelia
Oct.6, 2025

10. Lotus.

At the glossy quiet pond reflecting skies, the world, and
us within its wet, unmeasured depth—
to sit still, dazed in beauty, not quite asleep, perchance in
dream.
No sound, no murmur, no chirp or buzz: the whole world
stilled,
waiting for resolution, revelation, the inception of the
logos and the soul,
yet—one can still notice lucidity of airs, transparency,
utter purity of fleeting dreams.

And there floats a symbol amid the teals and greens,
earthly smells, undertones of browns and yellows: one
single bud,
alone,
trembling on the serene reflecting glass of pond—
wide open, pink-rimmed, pure,
white heart with presumed inner gold, not seen,
concealed in wide-skirted petals on the dark fluid
surface —

the lotus.

Stay grounded, calm, serene,
Absorbing her harmony and perfect form-
And then to guess,
and immediately know thy purpose,
and bow in awe
to the divine design of one's heart and soul.

Tamar Shengelia
Powell, Aug 29, 2025

11. Nasturtiums.

Some say they are a gift of a flaming radiance from
Helios to mortals
– The Sun's creative fire;
Some believe they to be Aphrodite's breath transformed
To orange-crimson blooms,
To fan the fires of desire.
Five orange petals – wide and plump,
Like lips open for a kiss,
Passionate; green arrow-heads for hearts,
And wide, rounded, elephantine leaves,
So succulent, so comely, so bright,
Contrasting all that surrounds them.
My lively, lush orangine beauties,
From grand orangeries of loving hearts.

Of Tamar Shengelia
Oct 9, 2025

12. Sprinkles.

Poem Sprinkles based on a Georgian folk song for kids written down by great Georgian poet Akaki Tsereteli.

ჟუჟუნა წვიმა მოვიდა,
დიდი მინდორი დანამა!
ვინც ჩვენზე ცუდი რამე სთქვას,
გული გაუპოს დანამა!

Sprinkles.
Why do sprinkles drop from the bright eyes of the shining Sun,
spraying happy holy tears on meadows of the emerald beneath?
May the vast azure skies
in sending sacred quenching showers,
protect this fruitful earth and us
from the grime of jealousy and malice of every cruel tongue.
Tamar Shengelia
Oct. 8, 2025

13. My Yearning Heart.

My racing wanting heart -
Folded onto a thousand fragile petals,
Pleated with hope and pain.
Light pink, pristine, transparent sheets,
Begging to be filled with blood-writings,
Wrought by labyrinthine, ornate words,
The strength and luster of bronze and silver dews...
Copious bunches of the bubbling, brooding
crimson juice of life and meaning.
And so, and thus, my heart and self could rejoice,
That we -
Strived, sought, aspired, created, lived.

Tamar Shengelia
Sept. 13, 2025

14. Poppy Gaze.
ყვავილების ქვეყანა

The beauty of your crimson blooms - poppies, drops of
fresh warm blood.
They watch me cut them down by sharp obsidian blade
thin as grass.
Deep black eyes shimmer accusingly - merciless,
immovable as time...
What do you see in me, your blooms color of my deepest
wounds.
I still carry in memory and heart your fields from my
childhood country,
Where the blood of your bright blossoms mingled with
lush green under sun's harsh gaze.
The splotches of the fresh red spilled in voracious battles,
skirmishes,
across the Georgian plains and lands...
I watched you sway as if wounded mortally, but intact in
your beauty –
you stand proud and grin, no survivor's guilt,

or maybe cry at night, in dark still mourning losses.
I remember so vividly, seeing you on the bright early
morning of my childhood,
pointing a tiny chubby finger and proclaiming-
"Mommy, Mommy, see! - This is a country, a kingdom of
the flowers!" –
"ყვავილების ქვეყანა!"
- Forever since caught up in magic of your blooms.
Citing a line from that famous song so popular, sung by
everyone then,
drifting through the air from celebration feasts and
tables, TV shows, radios, parades...
So, please, please, look at me again in this other land that
I dwell now.
On another continent, in other era.
Look to remind me, who I am and who I have become,
In heart of hearts, remained forever that three- year- old,
dazed and malaised by the magic beauty of the world.

Tamar Shengelia,
Oct.12, 2025

15. Immortelles.- Helichrysum, უკვდავა, бессмертник.

To Raj, with so much love.
Armfuls of bubbly immortelles, verdant,
Wide smiling at the yellow Sun,
I picked in the fields of emerald.
The golden glow of their bright blossoms
Caressed and lit your face,
Their blithe and bouncy neon sparkles
Planting smiles on thine lips and eyes.
A mellow breeze was spreading
The quaint aroma of the plants and grass;
Away in trees the birds sang gently,
While the cloudless blue skies,
Embracing the golden discus of the Sun
Were watching over us.
And I hoped thus –
At the end of thinning path of life,

Once upon the time when we become
This earth of fields, this scattered dust
Beneath some happy, careless couple's feet,
Sharing still in this bliss and beauty,
We, who ceased to be,
We, too, are and be the tiny part, a hue and hint
Of blooming bunches
Of the gleeful yellow immortelles.

Tamar Shengelia
June 1, 2023

16. Unsure Sun

Unsure sun plays hide-and-seek with clouds
In the transparent phosphor of the skies.
Dispensing tenderness and warmth of leftover passions,
Giving random quick embraces,
Cradling our faces, looking searchingly
Into the eyes half-shut from hushed
Glow of memories.
We sit on deck and discuss today and tomorrow -
Plans imminent and future,
While leaves in droves depart from trees sighing,
and reminding of beautiful fragility of passing hours.

Tamar Shengelia
Sept. 29, 2025

17. Irises.

Bruised by the sun's heat,
your purple petals tremble in the breeze,
its cool hand pressing poultice
to your paper-thin cheeks
and lilac capillaries throb,
pulsing from the golden rim at your core.

Caped and draped in purple,
you open to reveal a face
so comely, so calm, untouched by worry.
You gift beauty freely to the world,
to me and to passerby alike.
Your perfect shape brims with the essence
of strange harmony, tagging at my mind,
my imagination.

Since childhood, I have marveled
at your stems, your unruly heads
bowing in unison with the summer breeze.
I was forbidden to approach,

to touch- an evil stepmother
guarded you in her gardens.

And so you grew
more potent,
more mysterious.
Attracted!
Pulled and held in
frilly-purple haze of your gazes.
Still your form, your hues
bewitch me –
Irises,
forever etched
In the iris of my eye.

Tamar Shengelia
Sept.27, 2025

18. Rain, Rain, Go Away!

Rain, rain go away, come back another day!
My eyes are weary,
Blackened with ire, tired, yet not crying.
Salted rain is not expected, don't even think!
Rain – wink, wince from pain, and go away!

Rain, rain go away,
Come back another day!
Not today – I should be busy, easy, breezy –
Playing games with brains,
Picking words for poems, not tears.
They disappear when the pen is picked,
And words sip, pour
On and spill on lined sheets of tall grass
In outstretched fields – just windy wind,
Freedom - free in creation, free to fly or flee.

Rain, rain go away, come back another day!
I will call when it becomes unbearably simple and
mundane,

or not at all-
to ignore the verse and turn to prose,
or when hurt and pain churn the river
and spill it on the cheeks.
Eyes swell as brooks, and unbroken beads of silver flow,
Nose dripping with the yellow snot- so not pretty...

Neither harmony of words,
Nor tinkling bells at heaven's doors,
Just the boiling of the bowels,
A shaken, slackened core,
Tight ribs and a burning throat –
Sentences stuck like fish bones in the salivary glands,
The witnesses of my only love, confessionals and
Eucharist.

Rain, Rain go away!
It happens –
Happens to us, humans and poets.
We, the salt of earth,
Of strongest core of bronze –
Like stones thrown, to return
And hit where we expect the least – no cuts, but bruised
For remembrance
And the next verse...

Ah, verses...

Rain, rain, go away, come back another day!
We sing of rains, for rains,
of thirst and quench and nourishment,
for the coming sun's blinding brightness,
that squints in our eyes, tans our souls,
and feeds the heart with warmth and love.

I must sing about:
Rain, downpour, deluge with reign of love –
on my mind, always -
wished, hoped, imagined,
for when we stop being wolves to each other,
and become humans at last.

But that's another topic altogether.
Rain, please, go away –
And return with the sun,
Washed and dried, primed,
Portending the eternal sunshine
Of my cloudless mind.

Rain, rain, go away,
Come back another day!

Tamar Shengelia
Oct.7, 2025

19. Carrying The World.

The helix - pyramidal, earthen-shelled house carried on
your back, rocking slowly
While you steadily and purposefully climb greenish-
yellow blades of faded grass.
Watching you makes me ponder of myself and my
progress on the long path of life...
We share same slow gait, same rhythm, pace and flow.
A late bloomer too, delayed in search of self and
destination...

Yes, yes, I too am carrying my home, my memory, my
identity with me.
Wherever, any place I land, - starting anew, zeroed down
to nothing,
then gradually restored, self-propelled, self-sufficient like
salamander risen from the fire,
becoming me again for second, third, fourth, fifth time –
honestly, I lost the count...
Moving forth, so far from motherland, - I miss her
terribly at times,

alas a stranger there now, still foreign here, anywhere,
really...
the need to belong overpowering,
why?
- I don't know...

I foretell what your argument will be, -
you will casually say:
we are all visitors on this earth,
either parting water in a summer stream,
or floating high in transparent skies in short-lived
dreams,
and bathing in the luminesce of immense stars.

All starts and ends somehow, sometime, somewhere.
Thus, I surmised:
Those darkened helixes and pearly homes of slugs and
mollusks
mirror our own shell, cocoons we dwell and hide -
multichambered, attuned to common melodies and
tenderest of elegies,
- the harmonies of changing world.

Thus,
Move on, continue, don't stop, my lovely snail and carry
the weight,
Who you are and where you came from

housed tenderly and safely in your earthen cell.

My languid snail, proceed unworried!
We both somehow figured out such mysteries and
secrets,
That are so fragile to explain, too vast to tell!

Tamar Shengelia
Oct.7, 2025

20. Curly LiLacs.

Bows of curly lilacs, so lovely, fragrant, poised,
as if holding whispers of all the springs – past and
current.
Washed by pearly showers, they sway at the windows,
spraying hues of indigo and the palest ink.
Dressed in silk and perfume, they shake, prance, and
sing,
sing of youth, of carelessness, of simple joys:
running through gardens, playing hide-and-seek with
other blooms,
basking in the sun and ushering with winds of March
the gentle showers of the Aprils leading into
May's blooming warmth of colorful embraces.

Tamar Shengelia
Oct.12, 2025

21. February -May

To be conceived in youth and exuberance of summer,
Yet born in cold, in dawning snow, crispy frosts of cruel
winter.
To glow, blossom, doubt and hurt,
Questioning self and the world surround,
Encouraged, hesitant, alive with undying hope,
The dawn that breaks at last, sharp crystals of the past.
And in the third - final? perhaps - third act of life,
understand the flow and harmony and tune,
attune the aching, beating, wanting heart
to one - and only: noble, potent, elevated, soaring ART.
To take an ink from veins and spill
all love, all hope, all ache, all passion,
all that was absorbed and learned through the years,
hours of introspection and inspection:
in a sweep of long lashes of agate-cherry eyes,
in an airy cornelian cherry kiss on melting snow of
cheeks,
in a spread of black wings of eyebrows over tall smooth
forehead,

in delicate seashell wells of ears,
in over- steaming raven-smalt of curly tresses,
in that magic smile dissolving in sky-blue eyes
calling straight to heavens –
all, in full, all one has to give,
and feel that February may become one's May.
Yes, true of the truest myths, story-tales and songs...
When even brief snowy sleet rainy downpours blossom
into blooms and
Swift nipping winds shed new beginnings,
Dried blackened foliage swept away gathers in the
images of dreams
And early frosts transform into warmest glow of amber
embers.
Thus, my February - May Maiden,
may all Gods and Muses bless thee,
To inspire, soar and sing.
Live in love and peace with yourself, rule in the highest
knowledge, -
crafting, forging and creating-
proud, dedicated, wise, caring, jubilant, and undefeated!

Tamar Shengelia
Oct.12, 2025

23. Misericordia.

Latin "Miserecordia" could mean pity of the heart or heartfelt sorrow.

Upon the heart, the sorrow soft,
it lulls, it sobs, it bears aloft.
Through pearly drops, the spirit sees,
the wounded heart beholds at ease.
Misericordia, hushed the night,
Turn grief to mercy, dark to light.

Tamar Shengelia
Sept. 11, 2025

24. Mayfly Visitor.

My tiny visitor –
From a green leaf, so ladylike,
You may fly, my mayfly.
At first, I mistook you
For a butterfly:
Slim, slender, wispy,
A virgin with hair dyed
In neon blonde,
Thin wings of gauze
That spin and flutter.

Intrigued, after I watched you fly
On the shoulders of the gentle breeze,
I hurried home,
And searched your story - to find your days are
numbered:
I am amazed by your delicacy, your short-lived days,
Just one or two at most!

My mind ablaze

With the briefness of your beauty and
Your purpose,
Yet you care not,
What we think about you!
You begin as water nymph,
Lolling in a dew, with silver drops unseen,
then a subimago -
a dun, a pale teenager searching for
meaning of a purpose
with weak transparent wings,
a flutter, still half-hidden.
At last, a spinner, a lady in full attire
Of sparkling splendor
Ready to entice,
To give your life away for the next.

So delicate are balances of life
In our short-lived quests - a tiny life gives up its own
To beget a new one,
Even if it lasts a day or two....
A mayfly, I learned all about you –
A warrior with relentless time.

A tiny being trading her hours
For eternity.
How lucky we two, you and me
To share this kinship-

Your meager days,
Mine - stretched-out decades,
Both end in the same demise of life,
measured so unevenly, alas.

Tamar Shengelia
Aug 23, 2025

25. Seeds And Growth.

Grow silently, like a seed dropped into ground.
It slips into a crevice and lies dead asleep, dormant
till the first rains hit the fertile soil and swell it
with the springs crisscrossing black underworld.
A magic wand then swings and summons the energies:
Atoms, protons, photons, quarks of growth and so it
goes
in magic circles of birth, death, rebirth – living - dying...

One jinn springs forwards, nourishes, nurtures, sustains,
and blooms.
And the other – wilts and dries and decimates the living
into dust and soil
To be supporting the stubborn growth and development
yet again.

In cycles – call it
yin and *yan*,
or in Sanskrit the wise use a word –

Samsara,
which literally means wandering through, or running
around in circles!

Tamar Shengelia
Sept. 8, 2025

26. Arachne.

Arachne waving web of thinnest silk,
Adorned with silver pearls of the morning dew...
Its lace moves with every whiff of breeze and trembles
with a wave of leaves.
Light, airy net attached to the slinky stems of fragrant
mints,
Stretched loosely, reaching over heavy stomps of age-
darkened fence...
So delicate and ethereal are the works of the busy
master-weaver,
She herself looming in the center,
Poised, dedicated, calm,
Her daily duties done.
So are the tidy airy nets ready for an entrapment.
Such whimsical disguise is,
Arachne, - your artful trap of death.

Tamar Shengelia
July 25, 2025

27. What's In The Names?

Hibiscus - *Rose Mallow Pink,*

Lilac Crush Hibiscus, fresh airy, frilly flowers,

Rose of Sharon in bright, wide skirts,

Tahiti Rose, stretching necks of

Purple Pillar Rose, swaying in the dreamy haze,

Hibiscus Syriacus – the tender blooms of oriental lore –

all dancing flamenco with the breeze
On homegrown lawns.

Gatherings of pink, layered, frilly
Bottoms, or crimson layers flying in the air,
Bright and shiny in the sun.

Commonly called - *Swamp roses -*

51

their lace so large, bright, mellow
Arch their backs, heads held high-
The jolly smiles of garden beauties,
Prancing, bringing ease and comeliness to our eyes.

Tamar Shengelia
Oct. 5, 2025

28. First Light Of Spring

The hiding Sun plays peekaboo with clouds, beneath her
gaze
Generously spraying yolk of daisies, daffodils and
dandelions
On lush green carpets of the fields.
Thus, many tiny suns are looking up
To the true one in heavens,
Competing and completing her
bright image above floating golden bronze in transparent
blues.
The songs of birds, the breeze, the burst of colors in the
blooming trees –
This abundance, this lightness of the air, the fond
warmth of the Sun, -
nature gifting us:
the spring and stamina in steps, the smiles, hopes, plans,
living through these fleeting moments,
the unattainable art of being fully present, alive,
grateful, invigorated and engaged.
Now the spring descends, the energy of youth - may it

last -
As we still awash with the leftovers of winter chills, of
the shortness of the light and time.
The age and death are becoming distant memories,
As we restore, renew and seek rebirth.

Tamar Shengelia
Apr. 12, 2017

29. Skim And Stumble.

Flotillas in gray and black,
Round beady eyes - keen, unblinking -
Slice the glass of lakes.
Pearly necks and breasts, white underbellies,
skim the waters, reflections trembling on the mirrored
surface -
Graceful as long-necked Viking boats.
But on grass-bound shores,
they falter - heavy, awkward- dark, pink-splayed toes,
a wobbling, stair -step gait,
so unsure upon the waiting earth.

Thus, every living soul is destined
For his own realm:
Some thrive in depth of seas,
some soar across the skies,
some firmly stay ashore.

Tamar Shengelia
Sept 14, 2025

30. On A Rainy Day.

On endless rainy days ahead
protect me from the pain,
and these thinning drizzling tears,
that fall and break as heavy porcelain beads
at our soaked windowpanes.
Spread over us your wings,
a canopy, a shield, a refuge,
a shroud for warmth and safety.
Assuage my senseless fears...
Your kindness shines
Like thousand splendid suns!
That cannot be obscured
by these steely heavy skies.

Tamar Shengelia
July 30, 2025

31. In Between. Absurdist Prayer.

Verlaine – Romances Sans Paroles:
"Et tout reste est littérature". (All the rest is literature.)

In between now and there,
In between fear and a day,
In between heaven and my boy –
Have I chosen you, or have you picked my voice?

Never asked, neither wished nor/or imagined...
Away, out of my way, not in my way of things,
A hobby, not a business,
Or, other way...

Why or When?
Why You make me write?
What is the Way?
Which way You will lead?
And if I should follow –

Why?

In-between mind and hope,
In-between words and chaos,
In-between fragile Muse and
Atlas muscled, hugging the skies,
I believe You.

Look at me, Christ, look at me!
With your impossibly stern, loving eyes,
All-absolving in forgiveness and kindness –
Those absolute gifts of gray
In-between demons and pristine wide-winged angels...
Speak at me, to me, through me.

In between late bars and silence,
In between being lost and flowers
Nursed by this fertile, life - giver earth,
In between dogs and long hours,
In-between this skill
and all impasse, impacts, impossible things.

One glance, one ounce of hope,
One last breath of a mother,
one smile on yet warm lips,
one unbreakable bond with this cosmos,
and the newborns, one hug from my boy, one single love.

Elevated.
In between all,
In between one humbled life.

Tamar Shengelia,
Oct. 1, 2025

32. Origins Of Verse.

How would you write, you ask?
Trying to teach me a trade,
To instruct, point, prompt, define a task -
And I answer: *I lead with heart and live with heart!*

My pen in hand runs before my mind and writes the
words
That rang and sung within me hundred thousand years
before the time –
for a hundred thousand times again.

Then, when swans danced on placid ponds,
when rams glinting their horns scaled mountains high,
when tigers growled and fought with men in skins,
when the fair queen with a face and shade of the
brightest sunlight
was kept in citadel afar, when sad pale moon moaned in
clouds,
when oceans clashed and tore the firmament of earth,
when white doves flew to skies proclaiming omens and

salvations...

Yes, it was then - then my soul was birthed
somewhere near the nearest nebula.
She burst, bouncing off the darkness condensed,
straight into blinding brilliance
of cosmic waves and energies.
Since then, she sings and serenades,
the love and lust, the time and passions of the worlds,
real or imagined....

Tamar Shengelia
Oc.10, 2025

33. Gratia Plena.

"I am out with lanterns, looking for myself."- Emily Dickinson.

I am out with lanterns, looking for myself –
Nowhere to find the charms of childhood light,
The frilly ease of youthful thrills,
Neither too hopeful, not too wise.

Is it not enough – to feel alive,
Healthy, loved, cared?
Yes, more than that, yes:
So grateful for this aching heart,
For all experienced, learned, realized or not,
And lived throughout.

Gratia Plena!
For motherhood,
For every single second, long sleepless nights,
First smiles, first steps, first words, all firsts together.

And the pen in hand and scribbles on the pages,
For all awkward, heartfelt songs.

For every single hour,
For all - all, good or bad,
I offer the humblest, purest thanks
To you, my life, my fate,
So sweet, so full, so short and imperfect.
Amen.

Tamar Shengelia
Oct. 14, 2025

www.ingramcontent.com/pod-product-compliance
Lightning Source LLC
Chambersburg PA
CBHW060351050426
42449CB00011B/2926